# A SERVICE OF SHADOWS

## Tenebrae Service

## BY J. B. QUISENBERRY

**C.S.S Publishing Co., Inc.**
Lima, Ohio

9208 / ISBN 1-55673-390-9     PRINTED IN U.S.A.

———————————————

This service is dedicated to the memory
of Pastor Glenn G. Gilbert, who introduced
me to dramatic worship.

———————————————

# PRODUCTION NOTES

At the beginning of the service, 14 candles should be arranged on or near the altar with a larger "Christ Candle" in the center. As the Passion is read, these candles will be extinguished one at a time as directed in the service. The Christ candle is not extinguished like the others, but removed from the sanctuary at the proper time. When the Christ candle is returned, all candles that are lighted must take their flame from it.

The 15 readings may be done by several different readers to add variety and drama to the service. Three or five readers alternating readings works very well, or each reading may be done by a different reader.

The musical interlude may be vocal or instrumental, and may be decreased or increased in number. Selections from most Easter/Lenten cantatas fit easily into this service.

# A SERVICE OF SHADOWS

**PRELUDE**

**CALL TO WORSHIP**

> L. God said, "Let there be light;" but we still cling to the darkness.
>
> **P. We want darkness to cover our sins.**
>
> L. God sent his Son into the world not only to shed light upon our sins, but also to pay the price for them.
>
> **P. Let us then turn away from the darkness of sin; and in true, repentant humility, let us receive the light of hope in Christ Jesus.**

**HYMN OF PRAISE:** "When I Survey the Wondrous Cross

**CALL TO WORSHIP**

> L. The Lord be with you.
>
> **P. And with thy spirit.**
>
> L. Let us pray.

5

**PRAYER OF CONFESSION** *(In unison)*

Gracious Father, time and again we turn to the shadows of sin, and away from the light of your love. Forgive us Lord. Help us to turn away from the paths of darkness, and cling forever to the cross on which our Savior suffered and died for our salvation. We are in no way worthy, Lord, but trusting in the loving promise of your Son; we pray that as we hear the story of his passion, we may be cleansed by the fire of repentance, and made new creatures through his blood. We pray in the name of our dear Lord, your Son, who died that we might live. Amen.

**PASTORAL PRAYER**

**LORD'S PRAYER**

**THE PSALTER:** Isaiah 53:4-6

L. Surely he has borne our griefs, and carried our sorrows;

**P. Yet we esteem him stricken, smitten by God, and afflicted.**

L. But he was wounded for our transgressions, he was bruised for our iniquities;

**P. Upon him was the chastisement that made us whole, and with his stripes we are healed.**

L. All we like sheep have gone astray; we have turned every one to his own way;

**P. And the Lord has laid on him the iniquity of us all.**

**GLORIA PATRI**

**HYMN OF COMMUNITY:** "Alas and did my Savior Bleed"

# THE PASSION OF OUR LORD

## READING 1

The time of the Passover had come, and the 12 sat together around a long table in the upper room of a house in Jerusalem. The Master had told them over and over that this would be their last meal with each other. Yet none of the disciples realized what He meant. They were too earthbound to understand.

While they waited for Jesus to arrive, they began to argue once again about who was greater among them. In the middle of this squabble, the Master came into the room.

"Even now," Jesus must have thought, "you fight over trivialities! There is so little time left. My hour is so near! I must make you understand!"

Instead of scolding them, Jesus took action. He laid his robe aside, poured some water into a basin, and knelt at the feet of Peter, without saying a word. Disregarding Peter's protests, Christ tenderly washed the feet of his impetuous disciple. Then he washed the feet of the others. When he had finished, Jesus put his robe back on and took his place at the table.

The point had been made. They were to be servants, not masters.

*(The first candle is extinguished)*

## READING 2

Jesus and his disciples shared the Passover meal; the bitter herbs, the unleavened bread and the lamb. The conversation was not unusual. Then Jesus said, "He that breaks bread with me shall lift up his hand to betray me."

The 12 were stunned. One of them? Over and over they asked, "Is it I Lord?" They couldn't believe it. They knew

7

the old prophecies, but still, how could one of them betray the Lord?

Then Jesus said, "He that dips his hand with me in the dish, he shall betray me."

Judas, who had seemed distracted all night long, reached a piece of bread toward the bowl of lamb juices, and met the Master's hand at the dish. Looking up into the Lord's eyes, Judas' breath caught in his throat.

"That which you do, do quickly," Jesus whispered. In shock Judas stumbled to his feet and ran out of the room.

*(The second candle is extinguished)*

## READING 3

The 11 remaining disciples sat silently staring after Judas. True, he was not the most popular among them, but he had followed Jesus faithfully. Some of them even told themselves that the Master had probably sent the treasurer on an errand of some kind.

As they sat in confused silence, Jesus took a loaf of bread, broke it, blessed it and gave a piece of it to each of them saying, "Take this bread and eat it. This is my body, broken for you. Do this in remembrance of me." Next he poured some wine into a cup, blessed it and gave it to his disciples saying, "Drink all of it, for this is my blood which is shed for you and for many for the forgiveness of sins. This do in remembrance of me."

Thus it was, with the specter of the cross looming before him, that Jesus of Nazareth gave to his beloved followers then and now, the sacrament of holy communion.

*(The third candle is extinguished)*

## READING 4

As he sat in that upper room with his disciples, Jesus once again foretold his own death. Then he said, "I give you a new commandment: that you love one another as I have loved you."

Next, he told the 11 that they would all be ashamed of him and desert him before the night was over.

Peter's tanned face grew red with anger. How could the Master doubt his love or his courage! "I will follow you no matter where you go," the stout fisherman cried, "even if it is to my death."

Jesus smiled. It was a sad but loving smile. Yes, Peter would follow him to death, upside down on a cross, but not until the fisherman's hair and beard were white with age. "Peter," the Master sighed, "I say to thee that the cock will not crow until you have denied me three times."

Peter and the others roared in protest, but one look from Jesus silenced them all.

"Let not your hearts be troubled," Jesus said. "You believe in God, believe in me also. In my Father's house there are many rooms. I go to prepare a place for you. But I will not leave you orphans. My Father will send you a Comforter, the Holy Spirit. He will be with you always."

A little while later, Jesus and his disciples sang a hymn. Then they went out to the Garden of Gethsemane.

*(The fourth candle is extinguished)*


## READING 5

When Jesus reached the Garden of Gethsemane, he left all of the disciples except Peter, James and his brother John near the gate. These three went with the Master into the dark garden, until they came to a clearing. Here Jesus left them to keep watch while he went on alone. By a large rock, the Son of God knelt down in the darkness and prayed. Fear and sadness welled up inside of him. "If it be possible," Jesus prayed, "let this cup pass from me." But then he went on, "Nevertheless, not as I will, but as thou wilt."

This was not the way that the Pharisees dealt with God. There was no bargaining here. "Thy will be done," he said.

After he had prayed, Jesus returned to find Peter and the others asleep. "Could you not watch with me for one hour," the Master sighed. "Watch and pray that ye enter not into temptation."

When he had awakened them, Jesus went back for a second time to pray. "O Father, if this cup may not pass from me unless I drink it, thy will be done."

Once again Jesus went back, only to find the disciples deep in sleep. Disappointed, the Master knelt for a third and final time to pray. "Thy will Father, and not mine be done."

Strengthened by the Spirit, the Lamb of God was ready for the sacrifice. The disciples were still sound asleep in the cool shadows of the garden. "Sleep on now," the Master said softly, "Behold, the hour is at hand. The Son of Man is betrayed into the hands of sinners."

*(The fifth candle is extinguished)*

## MUSICAL INTERLUDE — Optional

## READING 6

Suddenly, the peace of the garden was broken by the sound of many footsteps. Jesus nudged the sleeping Peter. "Rise up," he said, "he that will destroy me is at hand."

As he was speaking, Judas entered the garden followed by armed men. Peter leapt to his feet and drew his long fishing knife. The others were also awake and on their feet now, blinking their eyes in disbelief.

Judas had told the men with him that he would point out Jesus to them. There would be no mistake. "Whom so ever I shall kiss, that same is he," the traitor told them. Now Judas came forward until he stood in front of Jesus. "Hail Master," he said.

Jesus took a step toward Judas and grabbed him by the shoulders. Judas paused. He was surprised by this and by the intensity he saw in the Master's eyes. Jesus seemed to be leaping into the lion's mouth, but why? That, indeed, was Judas' ultimate tragedy. He never understood.

After a few seconds, Judas leaned forward and kissed Jesus. Immediately, Jesus was taken.

Peter slashed out at one of the men with his knife. He would not let them take his Lord without a fight! There was a short scuffle and then the calm voice of Jesus rang out above the chaos, "Peter, Peter, put up your sword!"

The knife dropped at Peter's feet. Turning around Peter saw that his friends had scattered like frightened sheep. He suddenly felt very alone. He watched in horror as Jesus was bound and lead away. Why didn't the Master stop them? Peter knew he could have. It was more than the simple fisherman could understand. Afraid and confused, he ran into the darkness.

*(The sixth candle is extinguished)*

## READING 7

Judas and the others took Jesus away to Caiaphas, who had assembled the entire Sanhedrin in the middle of the night. The high priest wanted Jesus executed and buried before the Sabbath. Caiaphas wanted a fast condemnation so he looked all over for people to testify against Jesus, but all he could find was a handful of false witnesses. The judges of the Sanhedrin were not satisfied. They would not sentence a man to death on such shoddy evidence. There were even some among them who believed in Jesus. Caiaphas was getting desperate. The judges wanted to go home to their beds. With all the drama he could muster, the high priest stood face to face with the gentle prisoner.

11

"Jesus of Nazareth," Caiaphas thundered, "I adjure you by the Living God, to tell us if you are the Christ, the Son of God!" The high priest had called up the holiest oath in the Hebrew law. Jesus had to answer.

Jesus looked around the room with sadness. He knew what Caiaphas was doing. He spoke out plainly. "You say that I am," was his only answer.

Again Caiaphas said, "By the Almighty God I adjure you, are you the Christ?"

"You have said," Jesus answered in calm contrast to the frantic Caiaphas.

For the third time the high priest cried out, "By the Living God, I adjure you to tell us if you are the Son of God!"

The dark eyes of Jesus flashed. "I am," he challenged.

Caiaphas cried out and tore his fine robes. "He has blasphemed! He has blasphemed! You have heard him! Now what is the judgment of the Sanhedrin!"

"He is guilty!" they cried. "He must die!"

As Caiaphas looked on in triumph, they blindfolded Jesus, spit on him and hit him. They mocked him saying, "O Anointed One, prophesy who it is who strikes you?"

*(The seventh candle is extinguished)*


## READING 8

In the courtyard, a large, bearded man crouched over a fire for warmth. Or was it to hide his face? It was Peter. He was confused and frightened, but he had still followed Jesus to the judgment hall, all be it at a safe distance. "I have not deserted you as you said that I would," he thought, "I am still with you."

One of the servants from the high priest's household walked up to him. "You were with the man from Nazareth, weren't you?" she questioned.

12

Peter turned his face away from her. "I don't know what you're talking about," he grumbled.

"I'm sure I saw you with him," she persisted.

"Woman," Peter growled, "I don't know this man you speak of! Leave me alone!"

Another woman joined in, "He's one of them all right! He's a Galilean. The way he speaks gives him away!"

Peter turned to them and swore. "I don't know him!" he thundered. The words had barely passed his lips when he heard the cock crow. Horrified, he remembered the words of the Master, "Before the cock crows, you shall deny me three times." Ashamed, the strong fisherman ran from the courtyard and wept bitterly.

*(The eighth candle is extinguished)*

**MUSICAL INTERLUDE — Optional**

## READING 9

Just before dawn, Caiaphas and the others led Jesus to the gate of the Roman governor's palace. The prisoner's face was bruised and his robe was soiled with spit; yet there was a regal calm about the man from Nazareth that transcended the ugliness around him.

Pilate was uneasy. He'd waited all night for this visit. He'd even agreed to come out to them, since at Passover, no Jew could enter the home of a gentile. How Pilate hated this place and the strange religion of its people! But most of all, he hated and distrusted Caiaphas. Still, his hands were tied. One more problem and he knew he would lose favor with Caesar.

Pilate knew what Caiaphas wanted. He wanted this Jesus dead, out of the way for good, but something made the governor hesitate. Perhaps it was the serenity of the gentle prisoner, or perhaps it was his hatred for Caiaphas. The high priest was going on and on about blasphemy and treason, but Pilate was fascinated by the quiet strength of Jesus. Finally, Pilate asked Jesus, "Are you the king of the Jews?"

"You say it," was the only answer.

*(The ninth candle is extinguished)*


## READING 10

Suddenly a note was thrust into Pilate's hand. It was from his wife, Claudia. "Have nothing to do with this man for I have suffered much in a dream about him," it read.

Now Pilate was even more uneasy. Claudia's dreams had been known to come true. Pilate knew, however, that Caiaphas had to be appeased, so he took Jesus into custody.

Judas, who had watched the whole thing from the shadows, now burst upon the high priest. "You tricked me!" he cried. "I have sinned because of you! I am guilty of innocent blood!"

"What is that to me?" Caiaphas replied callously.

Judas threw the coins that he'd been paid for his part in the plot at the feet of the high priest and ran weeping into the early morning shadows. He ran until he came to a field just outside the city wall. In that field, the lost disciple hung himself from a twisted and barren tree. From that time on, the field would be known as the Field of Blood.

*(The 10th candle is extinguished)*


## READING 11

Pilate still wanted to avoid killing Jesus. His hatred for Caiaphas, his wife's dream and his growing respect for the silent prisoner made him unwilling to sentence him to death. So Pilate told the crowd that had gathered that he would have Jesus scourged. But even after he showed the bloody Christ to the crowd, they still cried, "Crucify him!"

Again Pilate spied a way out. At that festival, it was traditional to release one prisoner. Pilate gave the mob a choice. Should he set the gentle Jesus or the murderous Barabbas free?

"Give us Barabbas?" the crowd cried.

"But what shall I do with Jesus of Nazareth?" Pilate asked.

"Crucify him! Crucify him!" they chanted.

"Would you have me crucify your king?" Pilate mocked.

"We have no king but Caesar! Crucify him! Crucify him! The cry from the crowd got louder and louder as they chanted "Crucify him!"

Pilate saw that there was nothing left to do but to let Caiaphas have his way. Jesus would have to be crucified, but Pilate would not have the guilt on his head. He called for a basin of water. "Very well," the governor said, "He will be crucified, but I wash my hands of it!" Pilate dipped his hands into the water. "This is your doing," he said, "not mine! It will not be on my head!"

"Crucify him!" the crowd screamed, "Let his blood be on us, and on our children!"

*(The 11th candle is extinguished)*

## READING 12

The soldiers led Jesus to a common hall and there the whole battalion gathered to mock him. They made a crown of thorns and forced it down on his forehead. Blood streaked his face. The soldiers took his robe off of him and replaced it with a royal purple one. Then they mocked him and spat on him saying, "Hail to thee, King of the Jews!" But no matter what they did to him, Jesus remained serene, so the soldiers soon tired of otheir cruel game. They put his own robe back on him and led him out to be crucified.

Weak and tired from the abuse he had suffered, Jesus fell several times on the way to Golgotha. The soldiers began to worry that their prisoner would die before he reached Calvary, so on the way past a group of people, they grabbed a stranger and forced him to drag the heavy cross the rest of the way.

Two thieves shared Christ's fate. No greater humiliation could be visited upon a man than this. All along the way crowds gathered mocking and spitting and thirsting for blood. But here and there Jesus saw a familiar face, streaked with tears.

"Daughters of Jerusalem," Jesus cried out to them, his voice trembling, "weep not for me, but for yourselves, and for your children."

Among the weeping women, Jesus saw his mother, Mary. Her eyes spoke more eloquently than all of the weeping that surrounded her. She, too, felt the heavy weight of the cross. The mocking and the spitting burned her soul. The thorns that tore into Jesus' brow ripped at her heart.

*(The 12th candle is extinguished)*


## MUSICAL INTERLUDE — Optional

*(The sanctuary should be quite dark by now, and three "hammer blows" should be heard.)*

## READING 13

It was about noon when the workmen laid the crosses on the ground. The sun shone brightly, but along the horizon, dark clouds were gathering.

They stretched Jesus out on the cruel device and held him there while they pounded large pointed spikes into his hands and feet. When they were done, they hoisted the cross up and dropped the foot of it into an open hole.

At last the will of Caiaphas was done. Jesus had been humiliated, beaten and now he was hanging from a cross between two common thieves. Caiaphas had won. Or had he? If he had studied his Scriptures more, he might not have been so sure of himself.

Jesus surveyed with sadness the half circle of faces that crowded around the hill of Calvary. The pain of his body was only rivaled by the pain in his heart as he looked down on the hate that surrounded him. Turning his face to the darkening sky, he cried, "Father, forgive them, for they know not what they do!"

*(The 13th candle is extinguished)*

## READING 14

Jesus would speak six more times as he hung there in agony. Once, he spoke to his mother and John as they wept at the foot of the cross. He charged them to look after one another as mother and son. In this way he insured that his widowed mother, Mary, would be taken care of in her old age.

By mid-afternoon, the clouds had begun to close in and the mood of the crowd began to change. So Caiaphas and some others came back to the scene to stir things up.

"He saved others. Let him save himself if he is really the Son of God!" they mocked.

One of the thieves who hung on either side of Jesus joined in, out of desperation. "If you are the Christ, save yourself and us!" he cried.

But the man on the other cross called back to him. "Neither do you fear God, seeing that you are under the same condemnation? And we indeed justly, for we receive the due reward for our deeds; but this man has done nothing amiss." Then, the thief turned to Jesus and softly said, "Lord, remember me when you come into your kingdom."

The dark eyes of Jesus flew open. He turned to the repentant thief and smiled. Blood and sweat glistened on his face and neck, but his voice was strong. "So be it," Jesus answered, "I say to you that this day you shall be with me in paradise!"

*(The 14th candle is extinguished)*

17

It was dark as night now and the clouds rolled with thunder. The only light was a small glow about the head of the central cross. It was then that Jesus said something that delighted Caiaphas. Loudly the Lord cried, "My God, my God, why have you forsaken me?"

The high priest and his friends smiled with glee, but they would have been less pleased had they recalled the 22nd Psalm, which begins with the words that Jesus had spoken, and goes on to describe in detail the very things that Christ had suffered. Caiaphas and the others began to mock Jesus again in an attempt to stir things up. But the deepening darkness, the weeping of the women and the suffering of the gentle prisoner had changed the mood of the crowd. For many curiosity had turned to wonder, and mockery to fear.

Finally, the Old Testament prophecies had been fulfilled. The cup of suffering had been drained.

Jesus searched the crowd for Caiaphas, then, looking directly into the eyes of the high priest, he said, "It is finished."

Having said that, Jesus took a deep breath and spoke for the last time from the cross. He spoke as his mother had heard him speak so many times before, when he was a little boy, falling asleep in her arms back home. "Father, into thy hands I commend my spirit." Then, letting his head slump forward onto his chest, he released his spirit.

*(At this point the Christ candle is removed, leaving the sanctuary in total darkness.)*

So it was that Jesus of Nazareth died, on a dark and stormy Friday afternoon. As he breathed his last, there was a loud clap of thunder and the curtain of the temple that hid the Holy of Holies from the eyes of the people, was torn in two from top to bottom. It was finished. The Son of God, of his own free will, had suffered the worst death possible to pay the price for our sins.

**MUSICAL INTERLUDE** — **Optional** — *(A solo of "Were You There When They Crucified My Lord" is very effective here.)*

**CALL TO SILENT PRAYER** — *(After the prayer, the Christ Candle returns. Partial darkness is maintained for the rest of the service.)*

**PASTORAL PRAYER**

Forgive us gentle Savior. The darkness around us mirrors the darkness within us. Carelessly, we turned our backs on your light. Thoughtlessly, we have closed our eyes to your love and the sacrifice you made for us.

Flood our dark souls with your light dear Lord! Help us keep the images of your suffering and death always before us, so that we will no longer stray into the darkness of sin.

In true repentance, we offer ourselves to you, precious Lord. Make us truly yours.

In your blessed name we pray. Amen.

*(The Christ Candle returns, and the
sanctuary is returned to partial lighting)*

**HYMN OF DEDICATION:** "O Sacred Head Now Wounded"

**BENEDICTION**

May the light of Christ, who died that we might live, dwell in your hearts from this night forward. Go in his peace.

*(All depart in silence)*

*(The offering may be taken between the Gloria Patri and the Hymn of Community at the beginning of the service, just prior to or during the last hymn, or the plates may be placed by the door so the people may leave their offerings in them as they leave the church.)*

# ALTERNATIVE ENDING WITH COMMUNION

## CALL TO SILENT PRAYER

*(After the short silent prayer, the Pastor will say, "Amen." At this time the Christ Candle is returned, and some lights may be turned back on. Partial darkness should be maintained for the rest of the service.)*

## COMMUNION

**PASTOR**

Please kneel (or stand) and join me in a public confession that our hearts and minds might be prepared to receive the gift of forgiveness for which our Savior suffered and died.

**CONFESSION** *(In Unison)*

Precious Savior, we confess to you that we have sinned against you and against each other by thought, word and deed.

Like Peter we have denied you, afraid of the consequences of proclaiming our faith to an unbelieving world. Like Judas we have betrayed you, praising you with our words, but living our lives according to the world's rules instead of your Word. Like the crowd who cried for Barabbas instead of you, we have sought wealth and popularity instead of your kingdom. By our sins, we have crucified you again and again. We have not loved you with our whole hearts and we have not loved each other.

Forgive us gracious Lord! Have mercy on us! Through your Holy Spirit, cleanse our souls and fill us with the light of your love, so that we may become new creatures and serve you all the days of our lives.

21

**PASTOR**

Our Almighty and Merciful God has given us his promise that all those who believe shall receive forgiveness of all their sins. More than his promise, God has given us his only begotten Son, to pay the full price for our sins and to assure us of his love. As we have heard tonight, on the same night he was betrayed, our Savior instituted the sacrament of holy communion. He used the elements of bread (the pastor shall hold up the bread) and of wine (the pastor shall hold up the wine or grape juice) to serve as symbols of the price he paid for our sins.

Come forward now as the ushers direct you, to the table of the Lord. Remember his sacrifice, his promise and his Love. Receive his forgiveness.

*(The people shall go to the altar rail, leaving their offering in baskets at the front of the church. They shall kneel at the altar rail and receive the elements. As the pastor gives each person the bread, he shall say, "The body of Christ, given for you." As he gives each person the wine or juice, he shall say, "The blood of Christ, shed for you.' After receiving the elements, the people may remain at the rail to say a short prayer. Then they should return to their seats. When all of the people have partaken, the elements shall be covered.)*

**PASTOR**

In the name of Jesus Christ, our sins are forgiven.

**PEOPLE**

In the Name of Jesus Christ, our sins are forgiven.

**PASTOR AND PEOPLE**

Thanks be to God!

**PASTOR**

The Body of our Lord Jesus Christ and his precious blood strengthen and preserve you in the light of his love!

**PEOPLE**

Glory be to God!

**HYMN OF DEDICATION:** "O Sacred Head Now Wounded"

**BENEDICTION**

May the light of Christ, who died that we may live, dwell in your hearts from this night forward. Go in his peace!

*(All depart in silence)*

# ORDER OF SERVICE

Prelude

Call To Worship

Hymn

Call To Worship

Prayer Of Confession

Pastoral Prayer

Lord's Prayer

The Psalter

Gloria Patri

Hymn Of Community

The Passion Of Our Lord
*(Readings and candles extinguished)*

Musical Interlude

*(If communion is served go to alternate reading at this point in the service.)*

Call To Silent Prayer

Pastoral Prayer

Hymn Of Dedication

Benediction

---

**(Alternate Ending With Communion)**

Call To Silent Prayer

Communion

Hymn Of Dedication

Benediction

www.ingramcontent.com/pod-product-compliance
Lightning Source LLC
Chambersburg PA
CBHW071811020426
42331CB00008B/2457